ART OF THE WESTERN WORLD

PREHISTORIC TO CLASSICAL PAINTING

GIAN GUIDO BELLONI

GOLDEN PRESS   NEW YORK

ART OF THE WESTERN WORLD

General Editor   Marco Valsecchi

PREHISTORIC TO CLASSICAL ART

Translated from the Italian by Annabella Cloudsley

© 1962 Istituto Geografico De Agostini S. p. A., Novara

This edition © 1962 Paul Hamlyn Ltd - London

The paintings reproduced in this book were photographed by Studio Scala

Printed in Italy   Istituto Geografico De Agostini S.p.A., Novara - 1962

PREHISTORY

Prehistory is rich in paintings. We are accustomed to the symmetry of our own geometrical houses, and consequently we look upon rocky caves, with their natural walls made up of hollows and strange protuberances, sometimes smooth, sometimes jagged, as impressive but quite impractical dwellings. It is difficult for us to realise that the idea of building, first huts, later houses, arises only when natural shelters fail to meet certain needs. An increase in population can bring great pressure to bear in this direction. The change seems unnatural to primitive man—as, indeed, it is—and he adapts himself unwillingly to its artificiality.

It is surely most unlikely that the cave dwellers of Altamira, Lascaux, Ariège and La Peña Candano—painters of genius—would have been unable to build had they felt the need. They display remarkable manual dexterity in working their stone arrows. The precision, regularity and symmetry of the shaping are exactly right for the purpose, and are aesthetically pleasing as well as functional.

The cave, then, must be regarded as a dwelling entirely acceptable to the mentality of primitive man. It is decorated, usually with pictures of animals, but often there are human figures, too. The abundant evidence which has survived is obviously only a small fraction of what once existed, and we can be sure that not all the painted caves are known to us. Their discovery is often due to pure chance or a trivial accident. In 1940, two boys from the Dordogne, Ravidat and Marsal, with their friends Agnel and Coencas, were trying to rescue their dog, which had slipped down a hole, when they stumbled upon the Lascaux cave. But for this we might never have known of it. For the first time, processions of bulls, bovines and stags were seen on the walls in numbers such as to suggest the idea of a populated area of pasture-land, rich in thriving herds. Those scholars with some poetic sensibility, before plunging into erudite speculation, took delight in the imagination of a humanity which has vanished, yet is almost alive for us today as it is at Herculaneum and Pompeii.

Primitive man's first voluntary contact with colour, his intelligent love of line, his understanding of the manner in which design and colour could give form to his ideas, desires, or mere fantasies are incomparably more attractive to us than the painter who is most ingenuous and least touched by education nowadays, and who finds his crayons and tubes of paint ready and waiting for him at the shop. The primitive painter carefully controls his inspiration and corrects unsatisfying lines, conscious of the gesture he is making and the importance of his achievement. The significance of his work may lie in ritual multiplication of heads of cattle or merely in expression of poetic inclination. Because of his primitive state he has no critical judgment. He is free from all its fears and hopes, while creating profound beauty that stirs the spirit, and can recreate in the observer the artist's state of mind.

These murals appear unexpectedly to fill in the immense gap in our knowledge of pre-history. Their beauty and the talent they reveal in a period when writing was unknown lead one to believe that writing was not then invented because it was not really needed, since no additional intelligence or greater degree of civilisation would have been required. In contrast to art, which was a free outpouring of the human spirit, writing was a weapon in the struggle for existence.

EGYPT

Herodotus, the Greek historian, writes that Egypt is a gift of the Nile. Nowadays this assertion has an ironic ring, both dramatic and moving, since the river is being called upon to flood into the desert in the cause of feeding men. It is well known that the project will involve the destruction of many architectural relics but, in exchange for a few lost monuments, we shall have new developments in living. The archaeologist, who should be more aware than most people of the passing nature of things, will not be unduly regretful unless he loves the past only for its own sake. Such a man is not truly cultured: he is only erudite, subscribing to an intellectual, abstract vision of life rather than a dynamic, realistic one. The progress of civilisation is usually stimulated by an idea which can be expressed in a single line. The pressure of tons of magnificent monuments is hardly felt. So far as painting is concerned, this turn in the history of the Nile will not affect us, because the paintings are already safely entrusted to the care of museums or can be taken to them.

Egyptian painting follows the full sweep of its people's history. It makes its first appearance in prehistory; its last phase belongs to the Graeco-Roman period. The paintings of Fayum, for instance, came under Egyptian, Greek and Roman influences, and are described in various text-books under the headings of the three different civilisations.

As we shall also find in Greek painting, much Egyptian painting is on reliefs. These are almost always made of hard limestone rather than marble. Two examples are reproduced in this book, both taken from the tomb of King Seti at Thebes. Still more common are paintings on papyrus, especially in the *Book of the Dead;* these were placed in tombs where they have been discovered in great numbers.

Apart from their artistic value, the paintings provide us with an almost inexhaustible repertory of scenes from the life of this great people, showing us, in minute detail, the humble activities of workmen, bricklayers and peasants, as well as the ceremonies and actions, in peace and war, of Pharaohs and great imperial dignitaries, which in their range provide a visual history of this long lasting civilisation.

The Egyptians have a remarkably lively sense of colour, which is usually expressed in even, decided, sometimes quite violent, tones, but can also be delicate and faint. They love to juxtapose contrasting colours, in a manner which reveals not immaturity but deep feeling for the unique quality of each particular colour. They succeed in bringing them into play in a rhythm of such an original and creative character as to be practically inimitable. It is not by chance that forgeries of Egyptian paintings are the most mediocre imaginable. Effects obtained by working colours in the most subtle elaborations of tone and shade cannot be reproduced by technical skill alone. All this indicates that Egyptian painters truly understood the colours they used, adapting them perfectly to the demands made upon them by their individual environment, sensitivity, race, culture, and historical and geographical situation.

GREECE

In the opinion of the ancient writers, the Greeks achieved the same high standard in painting as they did in sculpture. In fact, they considered it a more important art than sculpture, which was itself always painted. Unfortunately, not even the slightest trace of colour has survived over the centuries for us to see. For the Greeks, a statue without colour would have seemed like a bloodless body, the mere ghost of a tree or a building, a nonsensical thing, however lovely. The natural colouring of marble, bronze or clay was no substitute for artistic vision, which sets itself the task, not simply of imitating nature, as Aristotle said, but of improving on it. Even in so unscientific an age as the Classical period, the human intellect was instinctively deemed superior to nature, and the colouring of even the finest marble could not equal that created by the imagination of the artist. Furthermore, painted statues and reliefs corresponded to the rounded view they had of art, being endowed with the characteristics they considered essential to artistic creation: form, design and colour. The rule seems to have been waived in the case of gold and silver— rare materials of exceptionally beautiful colour—but ivory and bronze were normally painted. Eyes made of glistening stones or jewels were often inserted, even in marble statues.

Despite the vast quantity there once was, little original Greek painting has come down to us. Ancient writings are full of admiring references to it, and we learn from them that Zeuxis, an artist of the fifth to fourth centuries, painted grapes so perfect that birds would try to peck them. The outlines of Parrhasius' figures were so realistically drawn that the observer had the illusion of seeing the whole body, though only part was drawn. Naturally, these are only epigrammatic observations, but it is clear that admiration was aroused by technical processes which any college student nowadays knows well.

It is a source of amazement for us to come upon such references in ancient texts, after the innumerable experiments of Renaissance and modern art which we know so well. Yet statements that to us today seem almost naive were then signs of profound though simple intelligence. We may find a parallel in the quality of the laws discovered by Archimedes, Thales or Heraclitus.

However, Greek wall and panel paintings have been destroyed, and only reasonably faithful and competent imitations remain. These mainly originate in the Roman era, and their survival is due to the volcanic ashes which destroyed human life at Herculaneum and Pompeii while preserving human creation.

Imitations of Greek paintings were particularly fashionable towards the end of the first century B.C. and during the first century A. D., when Hellenistic influences dominated Roman culture almost completely. Innumerable works of art were imported from Greece, and copies of Greek originals were also in constant demand.

However, we still have many examples—often of an excellent standard—of Greek painting. These are to be found on pottery, though it is true that in these paintings design tends to prevail over colour, which is the basis of painting proper. We have recovered large numbers of such vases from tombs in Greece, Asia Minor, Greek colonies on the shores of the Black Sea, and, in particular, in Etruria, which was very active in maritime trading and could easily import works of art from Greece. We have dug up so many Greek vases that we can trace the entire course of Greek ceramic painting, almost without interruption, from its first Archaic expressions (which are frequently imaginative to a degree unrivalled in the Asiatic world) through the Classical Age and Hellenism, to its ultimate appearance in Southern Italy. In the work produced during this last phase, there are signs of a certain tiredness and sometimes of decadence, even though examples of fine craftsmanship are not lacking.

Summing up briefly, it is true to say that the quality of Attic pottery soon became superior to work produced in other parts of the Greek world. The great beauty and variety of form achieved in so short a space of time can only be explained by the genius of the craftsmen who made them. At first, the artists tend to crowd the whole surface of the vase with figures and decoration. The style is simple, without being primitive. The figures are firmly outlined, in such a way as to define but not describe them, and the general effect is extremely vivid and imaginative.

Later, in the seventh century B. C., the undecorated part of the vase is painted black, and the figures also are painted black, but contrasting with a background left in the natural colour of the fine clay—often soft pink or yellow. On many vases the outlines and details of the figures are drawn by incising the surface. It is rather surprising how little difficulty we experience in accepting the black paint which is used for the human figures, since our frequent contact with more recent art does not prepare us for it, and it is not the most obvious choice of colour for the human image. Now and again, we do come upon other colours: red hair, a woman's complexion painted white, and garments striped purple and violet.

Towards the end of the sixth century there is an innovation, possibly introduced by the vase painter Andokides. Now the figures are left in the original clay colour, while the background is painted black. Details are also drawn in black, occasionally scored in, after the manner of the artists who painted in the black-figured style.

Certain names emerge from the long story of Greek vase painting: Exekias, Andokides, Oltos, Scythes, Euphronios. All these have signed their work. It is a convention among students of Greek pottery to call a particular vase or group of vases which can, on stylistic evidence, be associated with a certain artist, by a name derived from one of his figures. In this way, we have 'the painter of the Niobes', 'the painter of Penthesiles', or 'the painter of the fat boy' — names suggested by figures painted by unknown artists.

ETRURIA

Etruscan painting is known to us almost exclusively from the painted tombs. There is no doubt that public and religious buildings were lavishly decorated with a great number of fine paintings, but we are left with only vestiges of painted walls and terracotta plaques, which were either embodied in the structure or used as facings to tombs and other buildings.

The tombs were constructed like subterranean houses. Sometimes there were many rooms, and the walls were covered in murals. The Etruscans attached great importance to the sacred work of decorating and equipping their tombs, where they imagined their relatives would live after they were dead a life similar to that lived on earth. They gave the task of tomb decoration to the best artists available in Etruria. The painters strove to recreate in the dead man's new home a setting as similar as possible to his earthly environment; they reveal rich figurative imagination.

The gold and silver work is of great interest to the modern student, and must have had considerable rarity value at the time it was made, both for its beauty and technical perfection. We ourselves can only wonder at the latter. From the tombs also come many pieces of Greek pottery, some among the finest known to us, imported from the Greek colonies on the coasts of Asia Minor and the artistic centres of Greece itself.

As well as importing easily transportable works of art, the Etruscans certainly welcomed Greek painters and artisans from every part of the Hellenic world, since we have found works which could only have been made on the spot in Etruria. This theory is supported by Pliny the Elder (*Natural History*, XXXV, 152,154). The style of the majority of the paintings is patently Greek, but there are distinctive Etruscan features which can be attributed to native Etruscan artists in some cases and, in all cases, to the influence of local tradition. However, it would be misleading to speak of true Etruscan originality, since there is little evidence of this, whatever the fashionable interpretation may be. It would be more correct to define the Etruscan characteristic as local atmosphere, which is a sign of the taste of a people, rather than creative originality. It is true that Etruria does reveal irreconcilable differences of idiom, and, possibly, of temperament, from its foreign masters, particularly the Greeks. But it is also a fact that Etruria is the most important and consistent example in the ancient world of intelligent and elegant assimilation of a foreign culture. Moreover, the Greek influence is most evident in just those paintings and ceramic decorations whose character is Etruscan rather than Greek. This paradox suggests that Etruscan originality was stimulated by foreign example.

Our knowledge of history at the present time no longer allows the assumption that European civilisation is exclusively derived from Greece. Some of its branches have their origins in other civilisations. As contemporary thought develops along these lines we can no longer take the nineteenth-century view of Greek civilisation; it was then exalted as an image of perfection, but at the same time the view of it was too restricted. Greek art is no longer our only yardstick for evalu-

ating other art. Nevertheless, the characteristically Etruscan paintings are somewhat mediocre; they are far inferior to the Greek paintings, and, indeed, to work which must be considered to stem from the Greek. In a way, the relationship is similar to that subsisting between Tuscan and Umbrian art and original Italian works found in Tuscany and Umbria.

Etruscan painting very clearly reflects the various historical conditions influencing its development, especially Etruria's active trade relations with Greece and the Greek colonies in Asia Minor.

The first great influence on Etruscan art was the one from eastern Greece, which was dominant in the first half of the seventh century B. C., and filled Etruscan paintings with motives drawn from Syrian, Cypriot, Aegean, Cretan and later Corinthian traditions. In the second half of the seventh century came the Archaic phase, known to us through the quantity of excellent paintings found in the city of Tarquinia, which was to hold its supremacy in painting until the late Hellenistic period. The Etruscan centre second in importance for painting is Chiusi. Here, the work dates mainly from the fifth century.

ROME

Roman painting comes last in the history of art in the ancient world. During its long period of activity, from its origins until the end of the Empire, it may be said to have absorbed, to a greater or lesser degree, elements of practically every style of painting with which it came into contact over the vast area of Rome's expansion. It must be pointed out, however, that few Roman paintings have survived until now, though they are rather more numerous than the Greek paintings which remain to us. The majority were recovered during the excavations at Herculaneum and Pompeii, but others have been found, and are still being discovered, in many other places.

On the other hand, we have inherited a rich store of mosaic masterpieces. There is every reason to consider the art of mosaics as an authentic branch of painting, because its foun-

dations are colour and design. Roman mosaics have been found (indeed, they continue to come to light, as, for example, the recent finds at Piazza Armerina) in Italy, Spain, France, Switzerland, Germany and Hungary. There is considerable variety of style. Some mosaics are very different from the important group from Ostia, and from those preserved at Aquileia, in the province of Treviso. Other groups of mosaics of exceptional artistic and historical interest have been excavated in Africa (at Sabratha and Tripoli), and in Asia. The Asiatic mosaics show mixed Hellenistic and Roman influences.

The Roman paintings which are of most interest to us here are unquestionably those which reflect the dominant influence of Greek art, imitating its choice of subject-matter and its techniques. Earlier and more independent efforts are illustrations rather than works of art. We have already mentioned that most of the paintings at Herculaneum and Pompeii were imitations of Greek originals, or inspired by them. Not only Greek paintings, but also Greek statues, cameos, bronzes, gold and silver work, were much sought after by the Romans. Since so much of Greek painting was on walls, it was almost impossible to transport, and so it became fashionable to buy reproductions, or preferably to commission actual copies of famous Greek paintings by well-known Greek artists, most of whom are known to us today only by repute. This tendency was particularly strong towards the end of the Republic and during a large part of the first century B. C. Greek painters would arrive with their sketches of original paintings, which they would reproduce in the dimensions required by their Roman patrons. Paintings of grandiose, mythological subjects were especially popular. Then Roman painters certainly began to share in the work of reproduction and copying with their Greek masters, leaving greater and greater impressions of their Roman spirit and style as their work gained in authority.

In general, the paintings are intelligently executed, but are painstaking and not inspired. They have qualities which, today, will satisfy the archaeologist's curiosity in erudite problems; the cultured person's interest in grasping the meaning of historical relics; the public's enjoyment of images of perfection which it finds only in the past; and, finally, the artist's creative judgment. Artists are mainly drawn to the rather coarse, but robust and realistic, use of colour, and to the all-pervading sense of controlled energy, which are so typical of the Roman.

Side by side with the innumerable paintings dealing with mythological subjects, *genre* paintings soon make their appearance. These take their subjects from real life. We see aspects of Roman life, and, most vividly, the Roman landscape. It is fascinating to study in the work the reflection of Roman vitality and freedom of spirit in both form and content.

Roman painting, like sculpture, had great originality when it threw off the excessive Greek influence, which had led in the end to affected embellishments and beauty that was frigid. This originality drew its strength from a sense of actuality. Design and colour emerged, then, as an idealisation, not of an abstract vision of things and men, but of their reality. From what little of it remains to us we see that Roman painting has its own unmistakable stamp; we see, too, that it is not so much a continuation of Greek art on Roman soil as a genuine contribution to the pictorial art of all time.

THE PLATES

Plate 1—The 'Chinese' Horse. Lascaux.
Cows, bulls, stags and innumerable horses are painted in a side passage of the Lascaux caves. Some of the horses have been called 'Chinese' as a result of their build and the suggestive stylisation. The horse shown is perhaps the best known and most typical, as well as being one of the most beautiful. Of course, there is absolutely no question of an affinity with Chinese art, and only chance similarity is implied.

The short legs appear to trot along, supporting a round body brilliantly coloured in ochre and white with a small, narrow head. The short, thick mane is black, subtly reflecting brown, and wonderfully soft, shading off over the eyes and allowing glimpses of the shiny rounded forehead underneath. All the other parts of the animal's body are drawn in a fine and somewhat broken outline. This is typical of the Lascaux paintings. The granular surface of the cave makes it impossible to apply the colours smoothly, but, on the other hand, it provides an agreeable porousness, which greatly facilitates shading and the merging of one colour into another, and heightens the effect of solidity. Of course, it is still the actual application of the paint which creates the effect. The colours modify in intensity, become stronger or weaker, or indeed fade altogether, in a finely graduated progression, giving a curve or a hollow to the body, or an alteration of movement to skin or fleshy mass, just as the artist wishes. There must certainly have been a considerable period of experimentation in prehistoric painting before such results were obtained. Experience has been completely assimilated and there is no sign of mere academic diligence, although, taking the large number of painted animals into account, it would be reasonable to suppose that a good many artists worked in the cave, probably under the guidance of one master-painter or more.

To set the scene two bushes are shown, scarcely more than indicated without outline, the colour alone doing the work of description. The artists represents them leaning in the direction in which the horses are moving, and so adding to the illusion of movement. It is a very small point that the few bushes drawn—constituting the only hint of landscape in the Lascaux cave—are almost always shown bending in the direction in which the horses are moving. It is nonetheless an indication, however slight, of the dynamic quality permeating all the painting at Lascaux. As represented by the painters, the animals are alive in their spontaneous reflection of the psychology of the peoples who created them. There is no illustrative purpose here; they are as natural as a religion or a folk-song.

It should be understood that when we describe this as a cave painting the phrase is

Plate 1. *The ' Chinese ' Horse*. Lascaux (France, Dordogne).
Probably 40,000—30,000 years B.C. Length 1.40 m.

Plate 2. *Bull*. Lascaux (France, Dordogne).
Palaeolithic Age, probably 40,000—30,000 B.C. Length 3½ m.

explanatory, not pejorative: on the contrary, there cannot but be unqualified enthusiasm for the perfect correspondence between creative purpose and its formal realisation when we find it.

In order to give a better idea of it, we mention that the horses and other animals in the Lascaux cave are painted in a vast range of colours, so that blacks, as well as various shades of red and brown, play over the walls. It is easy to imagine what an extraordinary impression these splashes of colour—which are really, as it were, expressions of the artist's inventiveness—make on the colourist, especially the abstractionist, as he enters the cave. Perhaps they are even more striking than the design of which they are a part. There are also in the cave, alongside the animals, strange colourful compositions which could certainly be termed 'abstract' if we did not know that they had a precise meaning, not fully understood yet but almost certainly symbolic. The lower part of one of these symbols can be seen in our detail, high up where there are four vertical lines.

Plate 2—Bull. Lascaux. It has already been indicated in the Introduction that the discovery of the Lascaux cave was recent and that it came about through sheer accident.

At Lascaux the figures of animals—cattle, deer, bulls, horses, bison—cover scores of yards of rock. They are, one can say without reservation, superbly executed and sometimes of impressive dimensions, like that of an ox a good 5½ metres in length or, like the one reproduced here, 3½ metres. Others are much smaller and, relatively speaking, very small indeed. However, it seems that we should not think of these differences of size as being calculated with a view to a preconceived effect. A more reasonable explanation, and one that is often practically ascertainable, is that the painters—and there were evidently many hands involved here and at various times— were obliged to fall in with the guiding lines, as it were, of the natural rock masses. At Altamira the opposite happened, that is to say, the artist was able to exploit the natural

convexity of the walls in the interests of his artistic object in such a way that his figures have a physical solidity. But although this was not possible at Lascaux, the results here, however obtained, are most effective and give the visitor to the cave an astonishing impression. Contrasting with the series of little horses in line and with the horns of animals emerging unexpectedly from the tints of the rocks with a brilliancy of colour and liveliness of pose which are really striking, are as many more sudden masses of cattle, other horse-like creatures and bulls. One has a vision of almost ghostly animals, floating above the head of the spectator, for they are not always arranged on the same base line. But at the same time the construction of these animals is so natural that it quickly produces a sense of confidence. As you walk about this part of the cave, which archaeologists have called the 'nave', between rugged walls notched with thousands of jagged indentations, if you look up you will see passing before you a long procession of branching stags' antlers.

It has been noted that the style of the Lascaux animals does not show the same refined technical knowledge, the same level of creative imagination and of formal effectiveness that, in the Altamira cave, suggests a pictorial tradition going much further back. But even at Lascaux (which some place earlier than Altamira because of this lesser degree of artistic maturity) there is the same naturalism, a fine sense of tonal gradations, and a rare penetration of the psychological aspect of the animals.

Although it is true that a highly developed capacity for visualisation and the corresponding capacity for expression are only to be found after a long phase of high culture, no very precise rule can be deduced from this to help us in the dating of Altamira in relation to Lascaux. If there is a rule in art, it is that the appearance of an exceptional personality at a certain moment in a certain place is unforeseeable. Thus the difference in the artistic level of the two caves does not give us any really adequate means of establishing the relative chronology.

The detail which we show comes from the Great Hall of the Bulls, about 30 metres long and 10 metres broad. The enormous bulls seem to extend ghostly bodies, while other smaller animals gambol about beneath them.

The figures are painted on a calcite layer, which has a surface granulated with little crystals—a natural, very impermeable formation which has stood up to the passage of centuries. On this whitish background with many yellowish spots, our bull is outlined with the broad sweep of his profile deeply shaded. Evidently the artist sought to give the effect of physical size with this shading, used also on the body. A smaller animal, of a reddish colour, was evidently painted earlier than the bull by another artist, and their bodies overlap. But the extremely spontaneous nature of this painting allows for superimpositions of this kind, which would considerably reduce the value of a more sophisticated and perhaps more pedestrian art.

Just as at Altamira the bison were full of a gravity of their own, so the heads of the Lascaux bulls have their dark force.

Plate 3—Bison. Altamira. The cave of Altamira was found by accident by a hunter in 1863; only in 1879 was the presence of the paintings in it discovered by the twelve-year-old child of the archaeologist, Don Marcelino S. de Sautuola, who came across them while playing. It was the first cave of the Palaeolithic period to become known, after thousands of years of hidden existence; it is undoubtedly one of the finest of prehistory. It gives on to a height of calcareous rock and goes 270 metres into the hill, subdividing into naturally formed separate areas.

The detail shown here is from fifteen bison, both black and polychrome, which, with seven or eight other animals—boars, deer and wild horses—decorate the roof of a great natural chamber called 'the Great Hall', which is 30 metres from the entrance, at the end of a side passage which divides it from a vast gallery. The Great Hall measures 18 metres by 9 metres and has been called the 'Sistine Chapel of Prehistory'—an otiose remark which had already been made about the whole of Altamira. It is necessary to know that some of the bison measure from 1.4 to 1.8 metres in order to have some idea of the imposing effect of this 'herd without a herdsman'.

In the cave the roof is in its natural state, with all the variations in its surfaces which geological effects have produced. But the artist, far from letting himself be hindered by them, was able to adapt them to his creative purpose, using them as starting points for the shapes of his animals. In this way the artist has overcome his lack of plastic sense and has achieved a three-dimensional impression—perhaps by rather mechanical means, yet with the desired aesthetic effect.

Our bison, however, is one of those painted on a more or less flat background. Naturally this does not detract from its beauty; for art has the prerogative of disregarding hard and fast rules—it is rather that the artist has the privilege of imposing rules which he may from time to time discover.

The nature of the animal, the typical meditative solemnity of the bison, the massive agility of his colossal body, are realised subtly and with evident affection.

Some of the bison in the cave are black, but some, like this one, are polychrome. Experts in prehistoric art have said that the painters of Altamira here show themselves to be at the apogee of Palaeolithic art, and one must suppose that there was a long earlier phase when experience of painting was gained. These painters used as colours: wood charcoal, ochre and haematite, which produce reds, yellows and browns. But (and it is also in this that they reveal their consummate technique—technique which was itself an art in so far as it is of the essence of the style itself) the colours are varied not only by the thickness with which they are laid on, but also by means of scraping the surface (this is not always visible in photographic reproductions); scraping is also sometimes used to give particular gradations or to make certain parts stand out. Green and blue do not appear and as far as we know these colours

Plate 3. *Bison*. Altamira (Spain).
Palaeolithic Age, probably 40,000—30,000 B.C. Length, 2½ m.

Plate 4. *Rock Carvings*. Val Camonica (Lombardy).
Date uncertain, but between 9th and 6th centuries B.C.

were quite unknown in the Palaeolithic age, though we notice mauves, probably obtained from manganese. The effect is achieved by the use of few colours, but these are so well distributed that they show earlier experience in the art of painting as well as personal originality; this polychrome effect is a great aesthetic achievement. This is an art which can stand comparison with that of all periods and of all countries.

In this bison the reddish colour clearly predominates, while the profile of the figure, with its coat now bristly, now downy, is in a brown colour with clear gradations.

Plate 4—Rock Carvings. Val Camonica.
Prehistoric man not only represented animals but often men as well in drawing and painting, and was frequently particularly skilled at carving figures on rocks and in very hard stone. Besides, we must remember that there had been a long period before this in which craftsmen—for we must call them this when they do not really deserve the name of artist—were specialised in the working of the hardest types of stone materials. Naturally the workmanship seems even more expert when man had learnt how to use iron and to make tools from it. And this is exactly the case with the Val Camonica carvings, which it is thought can be attributed to fairly recent times, perhaps the sixth or even the fifth century B.C. Of course we are here in the realm of speculation, as now and then it is impossible to reach a really definite conclusion about such dates. At the present moment these carvings are the object of attentive study by both local and international scholars, and it is probable that fairly soon solutions will be found for many of the intricate problems; but, of all humanistic studies, that of prehistory is the most arduous, because of the lack of any inscription and of any written sources which might help us. This study therefore depends entirely upon the comparison of similar examples and upon intuition of the observer.

The rock carvings at Val Camonica form the most extensive complex of their kind so far known anywhere; they cover about 46 kilometres in the area between Darfo and Sonico. We must add that the love of cutting pictures in the rocks in this region was really a local tradition for many centuries. Indeed, we come across pictures and motives which make it clear by their content that they are the work of successive centuries right up to the twelfth and thirteenth centuries A. D.

With the Val Camonica carvings we are undoubtedly looking at an artistic phenomenon which, for purposes of definition, we may call infantile. Nonetheless it is art.

If by this word, at once so clear and so vague, we mean *tout court* the ability to express oneself by graphic means, the Val Camonica carvings are certainly art. But at this rate language would be synonymous with poetry—not a tenable opinion. So really at Val Camonica we respond more to the spiritual content than to the aesthetic aspect of this moving attempt at artistic expression, to the examples which it preserves of the imagination, symbolism and beliefs of a people otherwise unknown to us.

There are figures of deer, often accompanied by small, very linear representations of men, mostly in lively attitudes and often armed with shield and spear; whole surfaces covered with daggers scattered in disorder; then the solar symbol of the wheel; horsemen with enormous lances; the god with the stag's head (called Ceruno or Herne the Hunter in Celtic mythology); rows of men whose attitudes suggest that they are dancers; and, finally, other more or less obscure symbols.

Remote as the mentality which produced them seems, these carvings convey a strong impression of the men who made them. This instinct for representation reveals a complete break with art—which is itself no less deeply felt, but more consistent intellectually—and it shows us how a completely untrammelled beauty and purity may be possible. The figures are indeed scattered about without any order whatsoever, except for the general relation between one element and another—and even this is often inaccurate; so also is the natural proportion between the sizes of man and beast.

Plate 5. *The Goddess Maat*. From the Tomb of King Seti I at Thebes. 1312—1298 B.C. Florence, Museo Archeologico. About life size.

Plate 5—The Goddess Maat. From the Tomb of King Seti I at Thebes. This relief in the Museo Archeologico at Florence is to be attributed to the 19th Dynasty, and represents the goddess Maat.

The hieroglyphics scattered over the background fill the space as representational motives would; for their proportions, the way they are handled and their balanced distribution make them seem more like elements in a composition than signs with a meaning which may be translated directly into words. This is something one observes constantly in Egyptian art; we shall see it in other paintings reproduced in this book.

We shall look at the whole thing only from the aesthetic point of view. We must put ourselves in the position of the bibliophile who may value a book although it is written in an unknown language, enjoying its graphic and typographical beauties.

First of all we should notice the great feather on the goddess's head: it harmonises with the hieroglyphics, forming a link between them and the figure of the queen. The area occupied by the hieroglyphics has an atmosphere of mystery, because of the juxtaposition of motives like the two heads at the top, one in profile, one full-face—these are by nature explicit—with motives which are cryptographic and incomprehensible to one who is not an Egyptologist and who is therefore inclined to judge the work from a visual point of view. We should also notice how these elements, naturalistic and cryptic, have been arranged, and how well the interplay of objects and spaces, balance and asymmetry has been managed, conditioned as it is by the requirements of meaning.

The compact figure of the goddess, with her mass of lifeless hair, is as imposing as some monolithic structure; with the gentle curve of her shoulders and the rigidly symmetrical pose of her torso, she dominates the composition not only by virtue of her proportions, but also because of the aloofness with which she stands out, unassailable, against the shapes in the background.

As to the characteristic stylistic elements, they belong to the period rather than to the artist, who uses them as the conventions they are; but at the same time, with his instinct for form, he gives them his own unique signature. We notice especially the treatment of the eyelid and eyebrow: they are put in with stiff, strongly marked lines, in relief, and with an exaggeration of their size; there is a statement of the inevitable continuity of natural things in the firm, abstract lines. This is a very effective piece of stylisation, found not only in Egyptian but also in Assyrio-Babylonian art. It is a formula which accentuates the significant traits, leaving the others without emphasis. This occurs in countries with brilliant sunlight, where a plastic structure which was softly modelled would hardly be seen.

Plate 6—The Carrying of Grain. From Gebelen. The painting is divided into two areas by a horizontal band. In the upper part there is a motive of gazelles back-to-back, feeding from baskets; this has a perfect symmetry of design and movement. Symmetry is carried so far that the hind legs of the two animals are crossed in a way which seems rather artificial. There is undoubtedly a certain mannerism about it, but it is charming because of its restraint and the completely plain background against which it appears. The artist has painted with evident delight the gaily spotted coats of the gazelles; their outline is particularly beautiful, and it is enhanced by the way the horizontal line separates it from the lower section, where a donkey with a pack saddle goes on his way, followed by his master.

In the lower section, too, the figures are isolated against a monochrome tint, in the absence of any real background. This is a colouristic device which in technical language is usually termed 'a neutral background', and it was much used in the ancient world, even in Greece and Rome. It has, of course, its equivalent in sculpture, in those reliefs where the backgrounds are not carved at all, serving only to support the sculptured figures. In effect this means that the figures themselves are conceived of as existing in undefined space, having no connection with any surroundings.

The drawing is of the typical Egyptian kind: apparently rigid, but really having all the necessary flexibility, the subtlest vibrations and the easiest fluency. One notes little inequalities of drawing in the symmetry of the figures: inequalities which arise from the impossibility—and indeed the undesirability—of making an exact repetition, detail by detail; but, more than anything, they are there because the artist intended them to be. He shows himself in every way a primitive—using that term in the sense, unconnected with historical chronology, of one who does not know or feel that urge to artistic creation which is prompted by the kinds of truth which are learned. He knew, however, the profound truths of everyday life—truths which remain on the outskirts of a more highly complicated existence. In Egypt pastoral scenes recur very frequently because the country was utterly dependent on agriculture. But the creator of this picture knew well the rhythms of men, animals and things, and their forms really move. It is seldom that the quick, even gait of the donkey is so well suggested in Egyptian painting.

Below this scene are two dark bands, with two other horizontal bands between them, one white, the other of the same grey as the background of the fresco. This detail should not be overlooked; in the composition as a whole the arrangement of the border has its own importance, even if it has not the same significance as the scene. In fact it is often such details, marginal in themselves, which establish the central motive of the composition in its precise relationship with the colours and proportions of the whole. The division of the lower border into large bands establishes the scale of the donkey and its master; and it underlines the importance—psychological as well as representational—of the relationship of this motive to the area with the gazelles. This latter area is seen as light, lively and at once connected with, and detached from, the area below. This is the invariable sign of a developed sense of composition.

Plate 7—Papyrus. A Dead Man worshipping Osiris (The 'Book of the Dead'). Papyrus is a shrub whose pith, when suitably prepared, served the Egyptians as paper. Its use goes back to earliest times. Papyri are often painted as well as written upon. The silky, slightly rough surface, which takes the colours well, is by nature a light straw-colour, showing up the signs and paintings clearly.

The hieroglyphics tell us that the dead man is Neb-Qued. The figure under the canopy with the whip (an emblem of power) is the god Osiris.

In the detail from the papyrus reproduced here, it will be seen that the columns containing the hieroglyphics are divided from one another by lines. The ancient Egyptians read from top to bottom, so this is to prevent confusion between one column and another. It will seen that Egyptian hieroglyphics are in themselves a figurative element, like Chinese ideograms but with less scope for a personal style because they are less pictorial and are more in the nature of functional designs; they are, one might say, more realistic. However, both in carved reliefs and in paintings they often lend themselves well to artistic purposes, despite the limitations which their functions as signs impose. For Egyptian artists there is no real distinction between writing signs and drawing pictures, and this explains why the hieroglyphics are put right into the composition.

In this papyrus the columns of hieroglyphics are arranged in strict rectangles, in keeping with the spirit which dominated Egyptian art and which was characterised by the need to make the figures stand out decisively. This was a spirit quite alien to that important stylistic experience which has to do with undefined contours such as we see in Roman art, and which has had a development of the utmost importance in other historical epochs. But it is of course true that the whole landscape and the colours of the atmosphere in Egypt itself are very clear-cut.

The whole configuration is, even intentionally, one might say, without real symmetry. And yet every element seems to be laid out according to a rigid, almost mechanical,

Plate 6. *The Carrying of Grain*. From Gebelen (Egypt).
Tenth Dynasty, about 2100 B.C. Turin, Museo Egizio.

Plate 7. *Papyrus showing a Dead Man worshipping Osiris* (The *Book of the Dead*).
19th—18th Dynasties, between 1350 and c. 1250 B.C. Paris, Louvre.

system. It is as though there were a kind of concern lest the shapes and attitudes of the figures should escape from a position clearly indicated and capable of defining them precisely, exactly as it is laid down for them to be presented. All this has come to be generally defined as the ' hieratic quality ' of Egyptian art. This definition is true to an extent: certainly the priesthood and the despotic power of the Pharaohs had a profound and decisive effect on the Egyptian mind.

The artist often alternates intense and brilliant colours with opaque ones, applied with the tip of the brush, using diluted paint. In the figures of Osiris and of his worshipper, for instance, this clear but tenuous method of delineation gives added emphasis to the parts which are of greatest psychological interest, like the face, eyes, hair and hands. In other passages, as in the mass of offerings to the god in honour of the dead man—overflowing baskets, the haunch and head of an ox, a duck, etc.—the painter achieves an effective play of light and shade, despite the heavy outlines.

An outstanding feature of this scene is the contrast, almost habitual in Egyptian art, between the stylised treatment of human and plant life, and that of animals; the latter are themselves stylised, certainly, but are clearly pervaded by another, freer and more natural way of life. But this is a phenomenon with complex origins which could only be explained at some length.

In this papyrus the drawing, with its rigidity and its almost academic flavour, is less remarkable than the composition and the colouring. The linked but lively rhythms of the figure carrying the cup, the lotus plant, the accumulation of animals and things before the pedestalled throne, with its canopy from which a pair of eyes stares mysteriously— all these are impressive.

Plate 8—The Carrying of a Funeral Bier. Egyptian art shows a lively interest in pastoral scenes, in life which goes on in the field and which brings man into touch with animals. This picture really shows the carrying

of a funeral bier, but the scene has a countrified air. There is great liveliness of expression, even when the symmetrical and apparently mechanical rhythms seem at first sight to produce a monotonous modulation. There is, however, as in the detail we show, a tension of movement which only *seems* to be rigid: for the Egyptian artist tends to show with almost didactic and, one might say, symbolic clarity, the essence of the movement and the psychological state of the figures.

The same principle is at work here in the concept of the representational picture as in the writing of hieroglyphics; there, too, there are certain fixed elements which cannot be ignored, yet there is an extraordinary freedom in the way in which each artist in sculpture, relief, papyrus or painting has been able to preserve his own originality in the handling of them. It is really an education in itself to compare the same hieroglyphics by different hands and in different periods and to see how subtle and delicate are the differences which distinguish one from another. These differences indicate an originality which is not immediately obvious, but which is as integral a feature as are the characteristic tone-colours of different sounds. Egyptian art, certainly more than any other, exists between these dual demands of faithfulness to a prescribed scheme and the imaginative freedom without which no art can exist.

In the detail reproduced, in the upper part of which there is a frieze of large hieroglyphics, the composition is divided into two bands. The upper part has a recurrent spiral motive with large plants underneath; these, with their insistently repeated verticals, emphasise the sense of movement which the spirals give. The lower band contains figures, while the background is filled with other hieroglyphics. Whatever may be the functional necessity for their presence because of the information they give, they form, with their evenly spaced vertical dividing lines, a motive which gives balance to the composition, creating a vertical prolongation of the rhythm of the figures. One cannot give a rational explanation of this: it is impossible, and to try to do so is even in a sense to deny the inexhaustible resources of art; but this solution pleases and so has its value. We also see here the exceptional compositional gifts of Egyptian artists, especially in the decorative parts. These, it is true, may be the easiest to manage, but they are also those where it is easiest to fall into the banality of stereotyped and outworn motives.

A procession of young men, two by two, hold firmly with both hands the rope to which the ox is tied. Owing to the way in which the composition is arranged in the detail shown here, this ox is the imaginative centre of the scene. But it is incredible how, in any case, an animal tends to become the focus of attention; this is almost a kind of revenge which art imposes, confirming a law of the natural equality of living things.

In effect the great brown mass of the ox's body—with which the short skirt of the herdsman holding the flail forms a pleasing contrast—acts as the focal point of the entire representational part of the composition, since the other youths all lean towards it. It is a peaceful enlargement and extension of the scene after the serried rows of peasants. Their brilliantly white eyes and finger-nails stand out against the dark of their bodies. Their skirt-like garments have symmetrical folds and hang rigidly. This whiteness, which the lines of the folds seem almost to emphasise, creates what is colouristically a very restful area, after the bright vivid colours which are distributed fairly evenly. The whole figure area has the affect of a pause and has a special depth, coming as it does under the decorative zone which is busily filled with motives and colours.

Plate 9—Stele showing the Goddess Hathor and King Seti I. From the Tomb of King Seti I at Thebes (See Plate 5— The Goddess Maat). The two borders of the stele tend to emphasise its vertical character, while their glowing, changing colours unify the intense and circumscribed polychrome effects in the descriptive areas of the individual parts, each one distinct from the others. This is so in the blocks containing hieroglyphics, and in the clothes and their accessories, such as bracelets, collars and the knots at the waist.

The two figures are placed in relation to each other with a symmetry which is varied so as to avoid a merely conventional geometrical effect. However, the hands of each figure are in the same pose and this probably has something to do with Egyptian stereotyped ritual attitudes. There was certainly a habit of mind and body among Orientals—a particular suppleness and a relaxed arrangement of the limbs—which suggests a curved line.

As we are speaking of a relief we must not think only of the painter but also of the designer of the figures and of the sculptor (here all the same person) who gave the work its distinctive flavour. The style is a very academic one and shows a cunning use of all the technical resources and compositional methods. There is a sure command of effective motives, such as the clasped hands, where the fingers form a knot which is almost abstract; this is without natural vitality but very beautiful because of its concision. Up above, the hieroglyphics in their thick frames stand out like cameos in the composition.

We must also note the balance which is established between the two figures. The goddess Hathor, with the great symbol rising above her head, is drawn with dry economy, while the other figure is dominated by the trapezium shape of the cloak, which spreads widely at the bottom, in harmony with the triangles of the sleeves. In this way a balance is established without recourse to a mechanical symmetry; that would be an archaism of the kind that this work of art has left far behind.

In the upper parts of the stele there are less obvious but perhaps even more subtle indications of skill in composition: the goddess Hathor is slightly shorter than the figure in front of her; for if he had been shown as the same height he would still have appeared decidedly shorter, because of the enormous symbol on top of Hathor's head.

This sort of thing often occurs in Egyptian

art, which is often based upon minute interconnections in the balancing of masses; this balance often comes surprisingly near to the geometrical, but without fixity or rigid abstraction.

The artist had great command of detail but what is more important he had a formal elegance which is not to be confused with an elaborate and limp academicism: it is rather the manifestation of a well-assimilated experience of what was best in the art he knew, and of a very sensitive passion for clear, ordered moral beauty of form. We see his precision in the folds which run across the clothing in a delicately curving transparency; and in the hair represented in fine regular lines. But this last is often found in Egyptian art and no doubt has something to do with the Egyptian type of hair and the oils which were used to beautify it, presenting as it did a specific reality for the artist's interpretative powers to work upon.

The colours, as almost always in Egyptian art, are brilliant, alternating rapidly in contrasts which were evidently pleasing to a colour sense which is now outside our experience. This was known in the ancient world in Mesopotamia as well as Egypt, where the brilliant sun divides light and dark without creating any gradations.

Plate 10—Funeral Portrait. Fayum. In Egypt, even in Hellenistic and Roman times, it was the custom to wrap the mummys of dead people in linen, and their portraits were also painted.

This picture from Fayum, or rather from the Egyptian centre near the Nile where the majority of funeral portraits of the Graeco-Roman age have been found, has become famous throughout the world, because it is undoubtedly one of the most beautiful, original and suggestive documents from ancient times. The Fayum pictures, with their great eyes full of the profundity and sadness suitable to a funeral portrait, with their becoming quietude, the realism of their expressions and the very clothes, whose style and colours, especially, make them almost familiar to us

—these pictures often constitute real works of art, not always of great originality but of a very unusual pictorial sensibility which is new to us. The fact of being tied to the demands of a funeral portrait certainly creates a sort of monotony which does not give much scope for the play of imagination; but this does not inhibit that freedom, equally great in itself, which consists in handling with the utmost independence an artistic theme the outlines of whose treatment are pre-determined by strict conventions. Psychologically these pictures are not more remote from us than the Greek or even the Roman, being already permeated with that gentle acquiescence to fate which we find in Christian art.

The portraits of Fayum present the whole gamut of emotions: joy, sorrow, the carefree mood and sadness. But few of them are able, like this one, to communicate such a profound impression of the exhausted look of one who has died after much suffering. A few reached such a high artistic level that there is even a foretaste of Titian in the deep colours of the reflection, restrained but intense.

The woman (I was about to say the dead woman, for the pretence of life is funereal and melancholy) is shown with the bust slightly turned to one side and the head full-face, with well-arranged hair, two strings of beads, ear-rings with shining white pearls and an ornament on her head. The colour of the background, which has perhaps been slightly altered, is a rosy brown, which shows up the green halo around the face. Against this is the very dark hair, slightly waved and with a brownish shading near the narrow forehead, which makes it seem less thick there. The eyebrows, of the same colour as the background, make the forehead seem whiter and plainer.

But from the colouristic point of view, the eyes and the areas above them are of special interest. It is here that the artist concentrates his greatest creative effort. This is partly his own intention, but it is also true that we are entering a period in which in Egypt itself, or rather throughout Egypt and Syria, could be found the seeds from which Byzantine

Plate 8. *The Carrying of a Funeral Bier*. (Detail with two oxen drawing the bier). Egyptian. End of the 18th Dynasty, about the second half of the 13th century B.C.

Plate 9. *Stele showing the
Goddess Hathor and King Seti I.*
From the Tomb of King
Seti I at Thebes.
Florence, Museo Archeologico.
About life size.

Plate 10. *Funeral Portra*
From Fayum, Egyp
1st century A.
Paris, Louvre. About life siz

art would spring. Just as in that art, so in this painting—similar of course in this respect to contemporary sculpture—the eyes had a psychological importance unknown in Classical art. In that art it is almost always physical attributes which are used to characterise a person from the human and moral point of view. And they are often features which do not much express the feelings, such as the 'white arms' and so forth which we find in literature and which we also find under a different guise in art. This is an opportunity for saying that in the theatre the use of the mask, with its emphatic, stereotyped features, removed any reason for paying attention to the expression of the face and eyes. But now Greek and Hellenised man discovered the soul as it were for the first time, perceiving its vast, fluid, continuous life; what little of this was externally evident was manifest through the eyes and the voice, which of course could not be reproduced.

We also notice, as an indication of a realism hardly yet so much as hinted at, that the nostrils are slightly modelled, while the long thin nose itself is stylised in a way which denotes a disregard for the details of the face; this is in contrast with the eyes, with their carefully studied expression and colour.

Plate 11—Proto-Attic Loutrophoros Amphora. This is the motive which decorates the body of one of the most famous *loutrophoroi* (*amphora* used for carrying water for washing—sometimes ritual washing—purposes) of the eighth century B.C. The vase is 80 centimetres high, and its greatest circumference, which passes through the bodies of the horses, is 86 centimetres. Large vases are fairly common in Greek art. They give an immediate impression of magnificence which is modified by the strict sense of proportion which has determined their shape, so that they have neither the Oriental quality of Assyrian or Babylonian colossal pieces, nor the virtuosity, graceful and not grandiose, of some Indian works of art.

As it comes from Attica the style shows that it dates from the end of the 'geometrical'

phase and is already at the beginning of true Attic art, with its characteristics which are clearly differentiated from those of other parts of Greece. In general it shows an exceptional sense of proportion; a capacity to idealise figures to the maximum while retaining an extraordinary resemblance to reality; an uncommon psychological equilibrium, by means of which events, in themselves tragic, are felt and represented without any vague condescension. In this connection the figure of the *lekythos* shown in Plate 14 is interesting.

However, in this *loutrophoros* the features which will later be so greatly developed are only hinted at. But a keen eye will already detect that the silhouetting technique by which the figures are rendered lends itself to a lively and realistic way of portraying nature; for example, the widened eye and the well-suggested whinny with which the second horse tosses its head; and also the confidence with which the different parts of the figures are proportioned.

According to a method not despised by much later vase painters with a far greater range of techniques at their disposal, the painter outlined some of the figures with a deeply incised line; not all, however, for this was by no means a way of making the work easier, being done for aesthetic reasons. There are incised lines where particular importance is to be given to the outline of parts which are not silhouetted, as, for example, the horses' flowing manes, or where one horse must be shown as distinct from the one beside him. Elsewhere the painter prefers to use only the differing intensity of colour, as in the wheel of the chariot. It is perhaps even possible that, given the curve of the surface of the vase, the two shades with their varying brilliance (perhaps the same colour more or less diluted) are intended to indicate the curve of the wheel. There is certainly an attempt to render the three-dimensional nature of the hooked forms which decorate the area above the figures. The wavy streaks too, which can be seen at the top of this detail, are plastic and have been applied to the shiny surface of the vase with a similar intention.

Apart from the human and animal forms in the *loutrophoros* there are also motives whose function and nature are purely decorative. Clearly the earlier style, which modern scholars call ' geometrical ', persists in these vases. All the empty spaces between the figures are filled with these geometrical lines executed with such freedom that they are quite without any sense of repose. Between the horse's muzzle and the head of the charioteer there is a spiral motive, and between the legs of the horses behind the charioteer there is a piece of vegetation which is striking as a natural form amongst otherwise decorative and abstract motives.

But the whole effect which the figured part produces is predominantly a decorative one. The chariot is repeated all round the vase, amidst the continuous but confused dazzle of wavy lines, in a circular movement which seems to go on for ever. Of course, the painter of this vase was not the only one to conceive of this representational composition in a complex of figures and pure decoration; but among the painters of his time he is certainly one of those with the clearest concepts and the greatest ability to translate their poetic imagination into visual terms which match it in energy.

Plate 12—The François Vase. The detail reproduced is from the great complex of figures illustrating the mythological deeds of Achilles and Theseus; this decorates the famous bowl discovered in the Fonte Rodella district, near Chiusi, in 1884 by the painter Alexandre François. Although the bowl has been reconstructed, it is not in good condition; it was originally found in pieces and then completely shattered by a madman in 1900. Most of the colours are lost. (The figure we show, however, was certainly always uncoloured). There must have been a polychrome effect which was rich, not because of the number of colours, but because of their intensity; they are without any gradations and indeed have the solidity which was in keeping with the taste of that period, as we know from many other vases. From what we can still

see of the traces of them on the François Vase, these were lively colours, vividly contrasted in a way which is as bold as it is primitive. Some parts of the figures are also lost, but still the vase remains among the masterpieces of Greek ceramic art, and not only of the Archaic period. It bears the signature of Kleitias as painter and of Ergotimos as potter; they sign themselves as *Delineavit* and *Fecit*. The style of Kleitias is dominated by something typical of the Attic style: sobriety of ornamental design in the details and, in addition to a linear quality, naturalism in the drawing. But here the drawing appears to be pervaded also by a slightly Corinthian spirit, suggested by certain decorative touches.

Here we see only the figure of Ares; he is between Athena and Artemis, whose name may be seen written above the shoulders of the god. These figures are painted in black on a pale yellow background—the colour of the clay.

In the François bowl there may be seen, besides the stylistic peculiarities of the painter, certain features characteristic of the period. Incised lines are much used in conjunction with the colour of the figure itself: on the plume of the helmet, for the leg armour, the cuirass and the closely waved hair. The large round eye also belongs to the stylised manner of the period.

But here we must examine the work from the point of view of the poetic value which is appropriate to it; its elegance of design—which is not mannerism; the truly plastic power with which the muscles of the arms, particularly, and of the thighs are portrayed; the expressive vigour which the enormous dilated eye takes on; the energy of the long lean nose; the sharp outline of the heel and the natural flexibility of the foot. We do not wish to continue a catalogue which the reader will make for himself, but we note how unusual it is to see the back of a hand constructed with such accomplishment, with such real vitality, as this hand which holds the downward-pointing lance. Nor can we leave out the glossy quality which Kleitias managed with very few lines to impart to the cuirass which covers the god's chest and shoulders. These few lines, organised with a touch of creative genius, give a sense of the curve of the figure, not only in profile but also in depth—and this without the least colour, without any perspective cross hatching or shading of any kind—without, indeed, any acquired technique whatsoever.

To this must be added something which, given the tone of the figure as a whole, cannot be regarded as merely a piece of academic cleverness: this is the perfectly natural way in which the hero leans and sits on the stool. I would say that there is almost a touch of humour here, as there is in the whole figure, which represents a mature hero, who is perhaps getting rather heavy.

The vase is painted on every part, even on the outer surface of the long handles, on the brim and around the foot. Our figure belongs to the second of the principal bands on the body of the vase, where the return of Hephaistos to Olympus is shown. On the opposite side of the vase is the Trojan episode of the killing of Troilus. The first band, which runs round the circumference of the vase where it is greatest represents on one side the marriage of Peleus and Thetis, and on the other, which is the continuation of it, the procession of the gods paying court to them.

Plate 13—Lekythos by the 'Painter of Achilles'. The 'Painter of Achilles' is so called from an *amphora* in the Vatican Museum which is decorated with the figure of the Homeric hero and which seems to represent best the style of this artist; he is not known to us by name. One hundred and eighty vases have been attributed to him by modern critics. Many others are evidently by his school or by his imitators—their style is not so good and suggests that they are the work of lesser artists.

The term *lekythos* is used to describe a type of vase with considerable variations in proportions and dimensions, ranging from a few centimetres in height to 40 or 50 centimetres, or perhaps even more. Characteristically it has a rather slim cylindrical body and narrows at the bottom in the form of a cup;

higher up the outline broadens before narrowing for the neck, which has a high lip or spout. It has only one handle. Its appearance is often extremely graceful.

The white background of this *lekythos* is now broken up by many little bare patches where the surface has peeled, and the original whiteness is appreciably discoloured with pale blueish-yellow. But it is still possible to enjoy the clear bright colours which are the most unusual feature of the series of vases to which this belongs. This series is a rare one, which had few precedents and few successors; perhaps this was because in the Hellenic period which was soon to follow (we are now at about 450—440 B.C.) the use of colour was developed within the figures themselves and the background was usually painted in black. And one observes the total effect of the lively touches of colour in the chair, the transparent tunic, the glints in the hair and the free play of the lines in these vivid colours—now dark, now more diluted—on the figures and on the transparent clothes. It will be seen that the lower part of the body is clothed in a colourless gauze himation. Bordered by the two lines of key pattern often found in Greek vases framing the space used for the figures, the scene is an interior, a woman's room; this is indicated by a *lekythos* for scent, a looking-glass, and a hood which has long ribbons with pearls at the end. These objects, whose significance is clear enough, are placed above the figure, as are those in the Kylix of Brygos. This device is common in Greek painting—especially in the Classical period. Just as the use of words and phraseology was intuitive in the Greek language at that time, so artistic methods were intuitive rather than realistic.

In front of the woman is a hand holding out a helmet. We cannot see both the woman and the dead warrior (who is showing this to her) at the same time, because of the cylindrical shape of the vase. She sits in the chair in a pose which is lacking in energy without being abandoned—there is some liveliness in the placing of hands and legs. She is in a state of mind which is both fearless and hopeless, while all around is silence. For

this is, in fact, a scene of leave-taking by the dead: the dead warrior is appearing to his betrothed, to say farewell.

It will be seen that the atmosphere which we have tried to describe does not emanate from anything so explicit as the expression of the face, nor indeed from anything that objects can make evident. Classical art, still far from the expressiveness which was to come with Hellenism, was conscious of the feelings which stir the soul, but expressed them with great restraint by those slight indications which only prolonged study and knowledge of the Greek world teach one to recognise. The danger remains that knowledge of the subject will influence interpretation, but when this tendency is kept within the bounds set by critical standards, the art itself, opening up limitless worlds of thought, acts as an inspiration. Besides, there is no one way of looking at works of art. Aesthetic criticism is certainly one of the achievements of modern thought because it has taught us to examine works of art dispassionately. But it is not really scholarship to set aside all enjoyment of the poetic and imaginative, confining oneself to an exegesis which is too rigid and scientific, and sometimes too much taken up with the making of judgments.

Plate 14—The Phoenix and Briseis Kylix.
The picture shows the inner part of a famous cup (kylix in Greek) by the ' painter of Brygos'. The description of the painter, whose name is not known, has been formulated in the usual way by students of Greek ceramics, who connect him with the creator of thirteen vases, five of which show by their style that they were painted by the same hand. This style is to be seen in one hundred and seventy vases all together, from among which there emerge, besides the example shown here, a cup, with Dionysus among the satyrs, in the Louvre and another cup at the Museum at Würzburg. The ' painter of Brygos' is distinguished by the great liveliness of his figures and by his ability to unite exceptional vigour with great delicacy of touch; thus his figures are both impressive and graceful. His activity

declined slowly at the time when the ' Berlin painter' and the ' painter of Kleophrades' were reaching the height of their powers.

The picture represents Briseis, the priestess of Jove; she was the slave of Achilles with whom Agamemnon fell in love, so that he withdrew from the war with Troy. Seated facing her is the old Phoenix, to whose care Achilles was entrusted as a boy. Phoenix went with achilles to the Trojan war. It is clear that the painter wishes to show these two mythological figures in the time of the war, and to show them near or perhaps inside Achilles' tent.

At it is a circular cup; the figures are enclosed in a circular band, in keeping with the shape of it. This band has a key pattern, interrupted at intervals by a square containing a cross—a decorative motive widely used in Greek ceramic art; indeed it recurs with the utmost persistence. The success of this motive, which, with variations, is found in other forms of art, may perhaps be explained so far as ceramics are concerned by the fact that with its discreet alternation of light and dark, it breaks up, and yet at the same time links satisfactorily, the entirely black band round the edge fo the cup with the area inside the round frame, where the figures stand out in a pale yellow which is the natural colour of the clay.

It will be seen that the painter does not mind sacrificing parts of the details in the scene (such as the shield up above and the chair Phoenix sits on) at points where the circle of key pattern cuts them off. This does not matter at all: Greek artists—and this should not surprise us—were aware that beauty is self-contained and that its expression has no need of rationalisation. Thus the work of a fifth-century Greek artist of naturalistic tendencies offers what may be adopted as a justification of surrealist experiments and the metaphysic of modern art. The spirit is different, certainly. But every style has within it the principle of all others.

It would be completely wrong to describe either the shield or the sheathed sword between the two figures as ' hanging'. Really both are positioned in space in a purely

Plate 12. The François Vase. (Detail). From Chiusi.
570—560 B.C. Florence, Museo Archeologico. Height of vase, 66 cm.; height of figure, 9 cm.

Plate 14. *The Phoenix and Briseis Kylix*. Inner roundel of a kylix by the ' Painter of Brygos.' From Vulci.
c. 490 B.C. Paris, Louvre. Greatest diameter of the kylix, 32.5 cm.; of the inner roundel, about 15 cm.

Plate 13. *Lekythos by the ' Painter of Achilles'.*
Third quarter of the 5th century B.C. Athens, National Museum. Height of Lekythos, 27 cm.; height of figure, about 7—8 cm.

symbolic way, conforming to compositional requirements and not to those of realism.

As in the red-figure vases (see Introduction), the figures are in the colour of the clay, while the black serves for the drawing of the figures themselves and the spaces between them. It also makes certain decorative parts, such as Phoenix's tunic and Bryseis' himation, stand out. All this is in a black paint applied with the tip of the brush. The only real colour is the white beard of the old man. We see that the bull on the shield (the *Episema*, as the Greeks called these emblems) is painted all in black, in contrast to the figures; I think this is because the black figure admirably fills the space which the light-coloured disc of the shield creates; at the same time this device established the secondary nature of the bull's place in the scene.

Plate 15—Tomb with the Hunting and Fishing Scenes (*Detail*). **Tarquinia.** This fresco, which can be dated between 520 and 510 B.C., is perhaps the only example in the Archaic period of a scene in which nature plays the dominant part. In the other tombs at Tarquinia the human figures on the walls are proportioned in relation to the other features of the composition in such a way that their predominance is immediately asserted. Thus the vast extent of sea and sky here provides a pleasant shock. Yet the strangeness consists in a sense more in the way of representing the scene than in the scene itself. For it is clear from the other paintings in the tomb that these are scenes showing hunting, fishing and the love of the sea—the things which had filled the dead man's life and been his pastimes too. The gay and animated figures of the men seem to share in the inexhaustible vitality of nature. On the boat, whose prow is decorated with the lucky eye as a talisman against accidents, a naked young man is fishing and two others are making lively gesticulations. It is important to notice these narrative elements, partly because it is one of the functions of art to express them and partly because the critic is not entitled to adopt an abstractionist position—that is,

to judge them exclusively as forms—since apart from the purely colouristic or verbal manifestations of abstract art, there is no real division between form and content; and only the examination of content can ensure the validity of an aesthetic judgement.

That the painter of the fresco has a certain vulgarity about him is shown by the coarseness of the drawing, especially in the strongly marked outlines. Owing to the strength of these, the relationship between the outlines of the fishermen and those of the birds is not made clear in naturalistic terms. In fact, all have the same strength because the artist aims at a pictorially robust composition which leaves realistic considerations entirely out of account. With the usual conformity to the spirit of the period, but more than anything because of personal inclination, the artist, as a child will, emphasises the external aspect, the liveliness of the movements and the serenity of the atmosphere which is the keynote of the whole composition, rather than the spontaneity of the men and the creatures.

The sea, which is a green colour verging upon violet, stands out in clear contrast to the uniformity of the almost golden sky. The great waves which go right across the surface of the water are a convention for representing the sea which artists of the Archaic period used. For them the salient characteristic of the sea was movement. We notice the same attractive use of convention in the way the boat is shown on the waves, so that both its shape and the transparency of the water might be seen; a double requirement which the artist was able to fulfil.

There is a transparent shadow in the sea where the fisherman has thrown the lines of the fishhooks, which move slowly in the water. Unfortunately parts of the surface of the water are damaged, but the colours and the drawing are too lively and too personal for the enjoyment to be seriously impaired, and this fresco undoubtedly remains, if not among the greatest, certainly among the most moving and sincere expressions of Etruscan funerary art, simply because of the sympathy it shows for nature and man's relation to it.

To have a clearer idea of the painting and

Plate 15. *Fishing Scene*. Tomb with the Hunting and Fishing Scenes, Tarquinia.
Wall Painting. *c.* 520—510 B.C.

of the significance of the detail shown here, it is necessary to know that the painter, besides the boat and the birds, also shows dolphins dancing on the surface of the water, and that the bushes which can just be seen on the right spring from a rock where a young man is preparing to dive into the water.

Plate 16—The Lyre-player. Tomb of the Leopards. Tarquinia. This fresco can be attributed to the second quarter of the fifth century B.C., when the influence of Attic art was felt in Tarquinia. It was in a phase which, because of the seriousness which generally distinguished the subjects, and above all because of the unadorned intensity of the form which expressed them, is called the Severe Style. This style, which is well characterised, is to be found in works on the highest artistic and imaginative level in both sculpture and the painting of vases, in cut gems and coins.

In Tarquinia in this stylistic phase, there was a typical composition for tomb decoration: a banquet scene on the wall opposite the entrance, with musicians and dancers on the side walls.

In the Tomb of the Leopards the scene is clearly a copy of—or anyway closely based on—models of higher quality. The drawing is a bit coarse but it is not unacceptable, standing as it does between the academic and the popular. The figure beside the one we reproduce, for example (and I refer to it because it provides a good contrast and therefore sheds some light upon the one in this plate), is a tibia (a kind of pipe) player who is in rapid almost agitated movement. The feet and, particularly, the hands are really enormous—one hand is bigger than the face— perhaps to emphasise the skilful movement of the fingers, which run up and down the pipe. And one cannot say that the disproportion jars and is so obvious as to be intolerable.

The figure in the detail shown here is, however, much better managed. The impression of rather angular movement is a pleasing way of rendering a passage of music in pic-
torial terms which are also realistic. The attentive pose of the head and the facility with which the hand runs over the strings of the lyre is also pleasing. One notices a certain unevenness in the handling: how good, for example, is the painting of the fold in the front of the tunic, how stiff and academic that of the one at its edge.

The colours are really very well harmonised; there are gaudy shades of red and green which, colouristically, link the border of the tunic with the wreath of laurel on the lute-player's head. The figure is outlined in a light brown colour with certain parts in red, as on the bare left shoulder—a personal touch having nothing to do with the stylistic demands as such.

Details in a work of art have the same importance as the whole when they are examined not for themselves but for their place in it and when they are seen as subordinate; just as in a book we grasp the meaning better page by page if we understand the leading ideas of the whole work. With this in mind, let us look at the way the ear is painted. At first sight we might even be deceived into thinking it a rather clumsy simplification, but we must examine the form.

As we can see, the musician is moving between two shrubs, one of them clearly visible in this detail. Comparing this figure with others of the same type in the fresco, we see that the path they are taking winds in and out of the shrubs, and thus we are better able to understand the curious position of his body.

Looking at this fresco we can feel the enjoyment of a scene of merrymaking in the open air such as must often have taken place in Etruria. It was a world which knew the simple but deep joys of unsophisticated amusements, with everyone singing together in the open air. In Etruscan tombs, scenes of this kind are common, as they were in the rest of the Greek world, and as they were also in the Roman world, though perhaps with less refinement of arrangement and execution. There was a special taste, specially in Greece and Etruria, for adorning oneself without hiding the body.

Plate 17—Dancers. Tomb of the Lionesses. Tarquinia. This tomb, which belongs to the Graeco-Oriental school, may be dated around 520 B.C. on the basis of various archaeological and artistic factors. It has been inappropriately called ' of the Lionesses ' because of the two animal figures (which are really panthers) facing each other on the tympanum of the lower wall. This detail shows a part of the panther.

As will be seen from the plate, painting played the part of architecture in the tomb so far as features which could be represented pictorially were concerned: there is a column with a smooth shaft with dark rounded moulding below the abacus, which is brown, and a green calathus or basket motive. And in this connection we must remember that the structure and decorative features of Archaic architecture in Greece, Italy and Etruria were always coloured. A streak of the brown colour of the column runs below the area containing figures; and a large green band, intense in colour, separates it from a framework of lotus flowers. (The plate shows only the upper part of this.)

This plate shows the only one side of the scene, consisting of two dancers. We should take note, because it helps us better to understand the particular position of the figures in the frieze, that in the centre of it there is an enormous bowl, with a player of a tibia and of a lyre, one on each side of it. In the space opposite the dancers is a single dancing female figure, clothed and wearing a headdress.

The man is painted in brown, the woman in a light colour, according to a convention common in Archaic art. The outlining of the bodies is sometimes in black, sometimes in reddish brown, according to the colour of the body, whichever makes it stand out most. This outlining is, in fact, extremely important since the artist relies on it alone to give solidity to the figures. The third dimension is, however, lacking and its problems were not overcome until much later in the art of the Classical world. Then a completely new philosophic concept, placing man lower perhaps, but more realistically, gave rise to the idea.

The profiles are drawn in a way typical of the art of the last phase of the sixth century B.C.; it is a profile in which the slight curve of the forehead continues into that of the nose; from the tip of the nose to the chin it is lively and clear cut. In particular the painter dwells with a certain descriptive delight on those parts where his virtuosity may show itself, as in the waving hair and plaits.

The figures dance in a rapid rhythm which was orgiastic in the strict sense of the word. The term in present-day usage has acquired a pejorative significance which it never had in the antique world. We prefer to describe this dance as athletic in form, ritual in substance. There was no abandonment to an uncontrolled frenzy, but rather a strict control of posture which was the result of disciplined and persistent efforts. One sees this in the matching of arm and leg movements. There are also gestures with the fingers: in the woman this has a clear ritual significance; less obvious but certainly significant is the gesture of the man's hand.

According to the canons of Archaic style, the waist is narrow while the development of thighs and shoulders is emphasised in a way which was in keeping with the contemporary idea of beauty.

As to the general tone of the style—to disregard what may be due to the personality of the individual artist—we must not seek in Etruscan painting for the purity of drawing, the refined beauty, the noble and profound morality, or the subtle irony of Greek art. It was the product of a very different background, giving many signs of the Asiatic origins of a despotically ruled and rather obscure race. In this context Greek art became assimilated in a way which transformed its strictly rational basis into a sensitive vision. We must be forgiven if we use vague terms to define the extreme aspects of two different positions.

Plate 18—Homage to the Dead Woman. Tomb of the Baron. Tarquinia. The Tomb of the Baron—so called after Baron Kestner, who played an important part in its discovery in 1827—was painted in the last quarter of

Plate 17. *Dancers*. Tomb of the Lionesses, Tarquinia.
Wall Painting. 520 B.C.

Plate 16. *The Lyre-player*. Tomb of the Leopards, Tarquinia.
Wall Painting. Third quarter of the 5th century B.C.

the sixth century B. C.; at that time there were being introduced in Etruria the distinctive features and particular formal inflections of the Ionic style which Greek artists had developed on the coasts of Asia Minor. However, it has been observed that the paintings in this tomb also show connections with designs on Attic painted ceramics. But as the Ionic influence is dominant we may describe the tomb as Ionic-Etruscan. Of course the question of whether it is by an Etruscan artist or by a Greek working in Etruria is unanswerable. The paintings in this tomb, which according to some scholars exemplify the full artistic maturity of the Tarquinian school, present some difficult problems. A first question arises from the fact that we are not sure whether the artist regarded his work as complete, or if he left it unfinished for reasons which it is not possible to establish. Thus we should confine ourselves to appraising and enjoying the work as it is; this seems permissible since we are not judging the artist but the picture, whether it was completed or not. However, the fact that a new and unusual technique appears in this painting might incline one to consider that the painter regarded it as finished. Instead of the usual ground of white plaster, the painter preferred to use a grey ground in the area where the figures are. These are painted over the grey, producing a shadowy effect. The colours became absorbed by the porous rocks and have taken on that thick opaque colour which is the characteristic tone of the tomb. It would be rash to maintain that this innovation is an unqualified success. It may be that this was an experiment which went wrong; and even if this hypothesis is a simple one, it does not mean that it is necessarily mistaken. Indeed, the shadow behind the leaves—a shadow which is, in fact, a halo—is meaningless; and the fact that it might meet with understanding or even approval from us—hardened as we are to modern experiments of this kind—does not alter the reality by one jot.

However, it is the colouring and drawing that we ought to look at, and the distribution of the figures. The composition seems to be of an extraordinary clarity: simple, with a symmetry which is formal but is yet an integral part of it. Only a part of the painting is shown here; so that it may be better understood, it should be known, for example, that the alternation of the colours of the hose the figures are wearing, which here may seem incidental, is repeated in the rhythms of the entire frieze: a reddish horse with a rider in a black cloak; a black horse with a rider in red. Trees are at equal distances from each other, of the same height but branching differently in a way that is immediately noticed. This effective use of counterchange brings the frieze to life, avoiding monotony and yet at the same time not undermining the simple architectural monumentality of the whole work.

The plate shows a detail from the central part of the back wall. To understand the attitudes of the figures it should be remembered that they are moving towards a female figure (not shown here), who is certainly the dead woman—wife of the bearded man and mother of the boy. The man is carrying a great cup for libations and holding the boy close to himself as if guiding him with protective affection. The rhythms of their movements and of the composition as a whole are all close knit, like the symmetrical movements of their legs. The range of colours is light in tone and needs no comment. But I must recall again the psychological intensity of the atmosphere which surrounds the two figures, closely united in their act of dedication to the dead woman, in the fulfilment of the ritual gestures, the offering of the cup and the playing of the tibia. It is as if their movements are slightly dragging and one might guess that the father is gently urging on his son, who is hampered by playing as he walks. The stylisation, still archaic, is typically Ionic, as exemplified in the long profile and in the nose and beard; so also is the emphatically sinuous outline of the bodies. But this does not preclude an expressiveness of movement, though it be of a very elementary kind, and without any of the complexity of spiritual movement. But the great eye shines, luminous and intense, and shows the spirit to be deeply absorbed in the religious act.

Plate 19—Wall Painting from the House of Livia. Rome. In the time of Augustus, at the beginning of the first century A. D., there lived at Rome a painter called Ludius. Ancient writers attribute to him the introduction in Rome of the taste for a kind of art which had had considerable success in a Hellenistic setting. This new *genre* was landscape painting, with views of villas, gardens, woods and harbours, and it was only when it reached the Roman world that it achieved a really remarkable development. This was because it happened to coincide with the spontaneous inclinations of the Roman spirit. Paintings of this sort are particularly pleasing in subject-matter, and have a pictorial feeling which is full of attractions and rich in resources. They include the famous decorations of the House of Livia, sister of Augustus, at Prima Porta in the neighbourhood of Rome.

Since the evidence which remains to us is not complete, it is impossible to say whether this plate really shows a work by Ludius. But the hypothesis has been put forward authoritatively and since it is a painting in a villa belonging to the family of Augustus, it is extremely probable that it was entrusted to the painter who was considered the most famous in that *genre* in contemporary Rome. Anyway, whether it is by Ludius or someone else, the fact is that it is a really beautiful picture and, of its kind, it may be considered a masterpiece—a masterpiece of decoration.

The painting renders in artistic terms a garden which may have really existed. It is certainly like such gardens must have been allowing for individual differences. A garden in which the natural luxuriance was favourable to art and where certain fences and decorative constructions introduced a suggestion of order and the organised comfort of man, making it more welcoming and moderating the too great wildness and solitude of it. This, which in itself may be merely the art of gardening, here becomes representational art in the most satisfying way.

There is no human figure in the painting, which is made to live by its own vitality. In leaving out the human figure the artist shows a touch of aestheticism, making the subject emerge by virtue of the very richness which feeds it. This attitude was in keeping with the Roman feeling for nature, in which the painter sees reflected a sentiment which is really his own. The Roman loves nature deeply and loves her with that rustic background which civilisation has not obliterated; he seems to retire every now and then into a contemplation in which, unseen, he savours and absorbs her deep and ceaseless breath. It may be to a certain extent an academic reminiscence, but these paintings spontaneously suggest to the mind the memory of the *Eclogues* of Virgil, as well as the love which a man of such hectic political activity as Cicero had for the countryside.

In front there are fences of trellis- and of lattice-work; the second of these, standing further back, is indented so that it takes in a big tree. At its feet, in line with a continuous row of shrubs, is the beginning of a dense thicket. Many-coloured birds, fruit, shady depths and brightly lit areas are scattered everywhere. The painter is an expert landscapist, and his composition, besides being rich in prospects and colours, is pervaded by an exceptionally sane spirit. He is, for example, quite free from that rather morbid feeling which was to lead Romantics and Neo-Classicists to load vegetation with a quality of enchantment, giving the brilliancy of lacquer to the flowers and leaves.

The Prima Porta painting, the true work of a painter who took the subjects of his painting directly from the real life around him, and not from pictures by famous Greek masters of two or three centuries before, is among those works which show the qualities of Roman painting. It is painting which, from what remains of it, cannot really be described as very fine; even for the most enthusiastic and indulgent judges it remains greatly inferior to the Italian and European art of later periods.

Plate 20—Bellerophon with Pegasus. Pompeii. The picture shows Bellerophon with the winged horse Pegasus and Minerva, a mythological motive often depicted by Greek and Roman artists. In fact it may be seen on

a great many Greek vases, on Greek and Roman marble reliefs and in stone carvings.

This is a work of the best Roman craftsmanship, craftsmanship which is known to us chiefly through the secondary works of Herculaneum and Pompeii; it is obviously far from reaching the standards of the great Italian and European masters, yet it has its own robust character and a flavour between the academic and the popular. It is, however, able to give us deep emotions and to offer us something which is honest without being cheaply facile. There were far too many workshops of painters who specialised in copying famous works; for amongst all the academic and mediocre works, the good and excellent were lacking—though of course it must be remembered that many of the better works have no doubt been destroyed. Far fewer have been found in Rome than in Herculaneum and Pompeii, yet it is obvious that the most famous artists would have worked in the capital rather than elsewhere.

The composition gives the three figures equal weight, all three being involved in a heroic drama in which they participate with equally theatrical effect. Theatrical, because it is certain that the subject, which had been treated by other painters and sculptors for centuries, is here represented in a rhetorical way, and the enjoyment of the formal aspect of the myth has been substituted for the inner truth; that is to say, the subject lives more as a convention than because of its lingering traces of religious significance.

Pegasus and Bellerophon are represented in an impetuous rush upwards, the graceful white mass of the legendary winged horse acting as a background for the brown body and red cloak of the Greek hero. The goddess displays the golden shield and the helmet with the thick horsehair plume. The closely pleated tunic, thin as a veil and white with a blueish transparency, contrasts the artificial beauty which the Ancients prized so highly, with the two natural naked shapes. We must be forgiven if in this description we have used language which smacks of Classical preciosity; but perhaps the terms of the Roman art of rhetoric are not out of place in

explaining in the twentieth century a spirit which, in spite of all the academicism in which it has been wrapped, is full of feeling, intellectual toughness and aesthetic effectiveness—qualities which preserved it from the tediousness of later classical revivals.

In this well-managed placing of masses there is a whole coherent system of interconnections, of perspectives, of third dimensions, of the movements of volumes and lights, as in the hindquarters of the horse, in the chest and legs of the hero, and in the cloak which is stirred by his flight. In keeping with a tendency which one often finds in Ancient art, not only Roman but also Greek and ancient Oriental art in general, the painted figures have a sculptural quality. For although much sculpture was done, painting was more highly regarded. The truth is that the distinction between painting and sculpture did not exist as it does for us: it was simply a question of different techniques. There was just the concept of figurative art, in its simple but more comprehensive sense. Thus it was natural that there should be a tendency towards the pictorial in sculpture, and towards the sculptural in painting, without any incongruity and without our play on words.

Coming to details of expression, we notice the outline drawn in strong brown lines against a reddish background—an impressionistic method which had been unknown and which we find widely used in the many paintings at Herculaneum and Pompeii.

Plate 21—Comic Theatrical Scene. Pompeii. This fresco probably shows the climax of a comedy, but it is not possible to identify which. For one thing, very few Ancient plays have come down to us, and then it is more than likely only a generalised subject, since this is frequently so among other pictures of the same kind. Some vague derivation from the comedies of Menander has been suggested. (Menander was the Alexandrian poet who lived about the end of the fourth and the beginning of the third century B.C.). But this, of course, is a hypothesis which is not demonstrable. Side by side with great poetry

Plate 18. *Homage to the Dead Woman*. Tomb of the Baron, Tarquinia. Wall Painting. Last quarter of the 16th century B.C.

Plate 19. *Garden*. The House of Livia at Prima Porta (Rome).
Wall Painting. Beginning of the 1st century A.D.

Plate 20. *Bellerophon with Pegasus*.
Pompeii, Antiquarium. 1st century A.D.

—which is known to us only in part and often only by title—a minor literature flourished, to provide for the tastes of a countrified or suburban public. In the same way, one imagines, there were popular pieces which never reached the important theatres.

The figures wear masks as they did in the Ancient theatre. That of the man, with enormous lips rounded about a gaping mouth, a snub nose and the pupils, small and wrathful, starting out of the whites of his eyes—this figure is well known; it was reproduced in sculpture and in an endless succession of terra cottas. The woman, probably a lady of rank, has a mask with thin features and wears a kind of diadem on her hair, which is piled on the top of her head. The girl beside her wears a gown all of one colour except for the undervest; it does not reach her ankles. She is clearly a servant because of her hairstyle and the coarse features of her mask.

Leaving aside considerations of colour, the painter, who has perhaps a not very remarkable pictorial imagination, seems to give a competent and exact translation of the stage costumes. But what is really worth noticing is his gift of composition. He portrays so well, and with such penetration, the typical poses of actors on the stage—and we mean provincial ham actors. The restless gesticulation of the man and the somewhat rigid erectness of the two women seem in keeping with the rather crude comic sense one would expect to find in provincial Pompeii in Roman times.

Looking at Ancient works of art, so deeply interesting in all their aspects, it is always difficult to confine oneself to a purely aesthetic consideration. How interesting, for example, it would be to try to understand the states of mind represented here. The two women, standing close together, are clearly in alliance. The man, who is agitated because of we know not what insults already suffered, or fears of dangers present or to come, views them with hostility. The grossness of the man's paunch is accentuated and so is the thinness of the woman's face—a sign of ill-nature in the drama of all ages. Besides this, her affectation, the bad taste and the gaudy colours of her clothes, really belong to the stage type of a vain and backbiting woman.

The work is very well executed: the drawing has a certain delicate quality; the colours are well blended and there is refinement in the putting in of details. However, one must suppose there was an original which acted as a model for this, without being able to establish with certainty what the artist brought to it of his own. Perhaps only a touch of freshness and a certain thoroughness.

Plate 22—Venus Bathing. Pompeii. As we have indicated in the introduction, the paintings at Herculaneum and Pompeii, and indeed most Roman paintings up to the second century A.D., are almost always imitations or straightforward copies of Greek paintings, whether of the Classical or Hellenistic period. An examination of this present example convinces one of this fact as soon as one looks at the drawing, which is almost completely incompetent, especially in the breast of Venus, the outline of which is constrained and lifeless, and in the legs. The drawing appears inexplicably inept if one considers it in relation to the composition which, on the contrary, shows a clear idea of how to organise the motives, their interrelations, their scale and their positions in space. But the composition of a picture is easily repeatable, and this explains the considerable unevenness of the work. So far as the colours are concerned, although one cannot in this connection say the same, yet the model helps the copyist more than in the drawing, at least in that the essentials of it may be followed and reproduced more or less adequately. Besides, something of the copyist's own personality creeps into the colouring, which is often inferior to that of the model—but this is not to say that it has no artistic merit of its own; indeed, it often has. Thus, although it may be an imitation, yet even an imitation may have its own original variations: we are, of course, still dealing with second- or third-class art.

In this picture, however, the sense of colour

Plate 21. *Comic Theatrical Scene.* Pompeii. Fresco.

is on a level with the fine composition: free, restful, lively, as the theme demands. It is so, anyway, in the choice of colours, if not always in the details of the way they are used—but it is not worth over-refining upon this; it is so in the ease with which they flow and change, the considerable variety of their tints, the continual modification of their indications of recession; the indications, now broad, now infinitesimal, of light and shade. This management of the colour, transparency, and gradual and deep shading of the water produces an impression of the gentle coolness in which the naked body of the goddess seems to clothe itself. The very curve of the veil, blown out by a pleasant and persistent breeze, enclosing her as if in a niche, although it has a slightly academic flavour, has here a special pictorial value because it gives the effect of an apotheosis. There is a putto behind the shell, while on the other side (not shown here) a dolphin frisks on the surface of the water—a motive which is typically light and Arcadian.

Although we cannot call this a work of high quality, we see the charm of various details other than the central water motive: they are the curled hair, the shell-like veil behind Venus' shoulders, and the pervasive tone of happiness and repose.

Plate 23—Darius at the Battle of Issus. Naples, Museo Archeologico Nazionale. This mosaic, which represents the decisive battle between Alexander the Great and Darius, King of the Persians, is a copy of a famous fresco by Philoxenus of Eretria, a painter who was active in the last quarter of the fourth century B.C. The copy was made at Alexandria in Egypt, the centre of a flourishing art market in the second century B.C., and it was from there that the mosaic was imported into Italy and installed in the house at Pompeii which is named the House of the Faun because of a statue which decorates it. The mosaic was placed in the floor of the house and so is seen from above as its perspective demands.

As it is a copy, this mosaic, like the other paintings from Pompeii and Herculaneum illustrated in this book, must be considered from the point of view of colour and composition and with, as it were, a tempered judgment. There is no use dwelling on those uncertainties, those defects which are typical of copyists' work; we will just point out the general—but not very great—hardness of the drawing, which is the fatal result of the effort to keep close to the original. This mosaic is certainly scrupulously faithful; it is enough to look, for example, at the restless movement of the highlights on the horses' coats as the muscles tighten in the effort of flight.

The scene is imagined as being lit from the front by the sun, as is shown by the way the light and shade fall on the faces of the warriors. This lighting involved for the artist (and for the craftsmen who made the copy) a careful study of the disposition of light and shade throughout the whole of the large mosaic. This task was not easy but extremely important in a work such as this, where considerations of design, colour and form, spiritual and descriptive values, states of mind and the instinctive movements of bodies, all these elements play an equal part in a totality which is unambiguous, coherent and harmonious throughout.

The conception of the composition is imposing and the detail shown must not be thought of as representing it adequately, since the scene as a whole is sustained by a masterly poetic energy, with a corresponding breadth and complexity of colouristic ideas. But this detail certainly shows the dramatic turmoil at its most intense; it is here therefore—since in a masterpiece there is no difference between form and content—that the forms in all their elements: design, colour, attitude, movement, concentrate their greatest expression and their most profound significance.

The lack of a background—the scene takes place in an indeterminate space, without landscape or sky—reflects the Classical habit of ignoring nature except when it was an integral part of the subject; it was represented sparingly and in an almost symbolic way. For example, in the Garden of the Hesperides a tree is enough to indicate the surroundings. But in this Alexander and Darius mosaic the background is completely empty, 'neutral' as we say in technical language; thus it centres all the dramatic frenzy in the isolated confusion of the struggle.

There are accurate portrayals of the details of the horses' harness and of the warriors' costumes (valuable archaeological evidence of their style and colour), elements which over and above their objective reality play their part in the compositional and colouristic whole. Apart from these, the strong foreshortening of the horses in the wild jostling of their bodies, which the reins can hardly control, is striking. And in the same way, at the apex, as it were, both formally and psychologically, is the group of Persian warriors' heads, their faces contorted by the excitement of battle, seen amidst the criss-cross of lances. Finally, there is the heart-rending passage showing the fallen warrior under the horses' hooves. His terror is expressed in his eyes and open mouth and in the hunching of his shoulders.

Plate 24—Pavement Mosaic. Piazza Armerina. Some decades ago the pavement mosaic known as the *Eraclia* (because it shows the labours and triumph of Hercules) was discovered in the Casale region, southwest of the little town of Piazza Armerina in Sicily. But it was only in 1950 that the mosaics illustrated here came to light during the large-scale excavations directed by Gino Vincio Gentili for the Soprintendenza alle Antichità della Sicilia Orientale. They immediately became famous, and constitute the largest complex of Roman mosaic art to be unearthed in Italy.

The mosaics have both mythological and real-life subjects. Of course such a vast complex is not the work of one artist; the mosaic technique itself involves the work of many craftsmen, who inevitably have varying inclinations and abilities. But the mosaics of Piazza Armerina are in every case on a remarkably high artistic level, appealing both to the art lover seeking only beauty and an immediate emotion, and to the archaeologist and art critic, who ponder on beauty in history and in the thought of mankind.

The detail shown here comes from the floor, which extends over the whole area of a large rectangular chamber, 20 metres by 4, with apses in the short sides. It represents the Circus Maximus at Rome with a chariot race. The two young men in the detail are hailing the arrival of the winning chariot, one playing a trumpet, the other waving a palm branch. One of the winning horses' hooves can be seen on the right. The detail is certainly not enough to give any idea of the immense mosaic, which really needs many plates to illustrate it—much more than are allowed by the scope of this book, which is intended only to give the reader his bearings. However, it is enough, in the context of these brief notes on Ancient painting, to clarify important problems of style and artistic tendency. For the two figures show very well certain aesthetic principles which became established at the end of the third and beginning of the fourth centuries A.D., this being the period at which there is reason to believe they were executed.

First of all we must notice the technique, which involves the use of exceptionally large pieces of mosaic—certainly larger than those one sees in other examples of Roman mosaic art. Naturally the size of these *tesserae*, as they are called, has to be in proportion to the size of the mosaic as a whole. We shall also see that there is not a trace here of that sort of affectation which made for the choice of really minute *tesserae* in mosaics of the early Imperial period: the whole style of the Piazza Armerina mosaic is utterly different.

As a characteristic of the method, we note that there is a band of three rows of *tesserae* which follow exactly the profile of the figures, thus emphasising their outlines and avoiding any danger of encroaching upon them.

But above all we must emphasise the particular structure of form which the figures show. Here there is no suggestion at all of that system of harmony and proportion which the Greeks discovered. Instead of the balance of parts, instead of a representation conceived of in such terms that the images created appear as the most perfect formulation which could possibly arise from the reality—instead of all

Plate 22. *Venus Bathing*. House of Venus, Pompeii.
Wall painting. 1st century A.D.

this we have a conception which denies the importance of the external aspect of things, people or animals. Not that either Greek or Roman art—needless to say—were, before this, entirely preoccupied with externals. But the external aspects of things were regarded as being at one with their essence. Now, on the contrary, with the decline of the view of man as superior to all things, there was almost a pleasure in making the external aspect humble. But to compensate for this a much wider range of spiritual and psychological phenomena became the themes of Roman art

at the time of the decline of the Empire.

One is struck by the fact that the proportions of the figures do not follow the canons of aesthetic beauty; one must rather look for intense expressiveness in the faces, as in the horn player with eyes fixed ahead of him, ignoring his surroundings the better to concentrate on playing the right notes. The proportions conform to the same rules. Proportion in the Classical sense is ignored. The figures are short and squat and yet very effective. In Roman art the way which leads to the early Middle Ages is already clear.

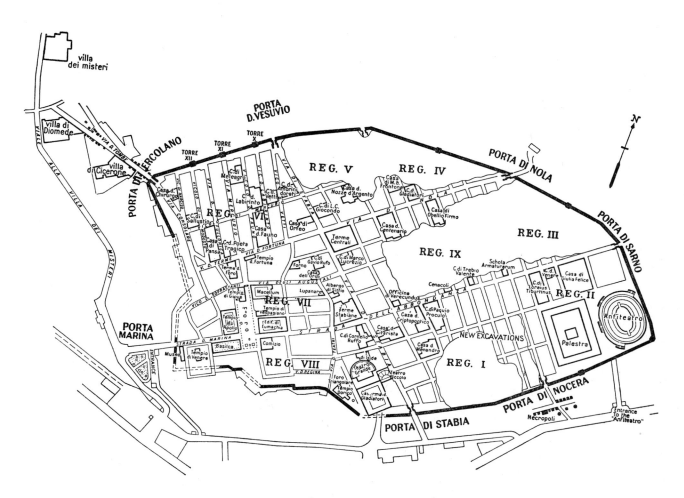

Street map of Pompeii

Plate 24. *Youths acclaiming the winning chariot at the Circus Maximus, Rome.*
Piazza Armerina (Sicily).   Mosaic.   4th century A.D.

Plate 23. *Darius at the Battle of Issus*. Detail of the Alexander Mosaic.
2nd century B.C.   From the House of the Faun, Pompeii.
Naples, Museo Archeologico Nazionale.   Height, almost 3 m.

APPENDIX - Notes of method

Roman Painting

The paintings found in Pompeii and Herculaneum are in a remarkable state of preservation.

It is known that these range over a period of two hundred years, and they, not surprisingly, include a number of different techniques. We have only imperfect knowledge of most of these, although the term ' fresco ' is commonly applied to them all. Properly ' fresco ' refers to wall painting done in wet lime plaster. This is true fresco (*fresco buono*) and is a very limiting and difficult process suited only to certain climates and demanding great technical ability. Done properly it is a permanent method with considerable attraction. *Fresco secco* is a method of painting on a lime plaster which has set. Since it is bound to the plaster and not incorporated into its structure, *fresco secco* does not usually have the same permanence. Both these methods appear to have been used with others in combination. The method in which it is generally believed that most of the Pompeian frescoes were painted is known as *stucco lustro*, but there is the possibility that an encaustic, or heated wax, process was used. The peculiarly hard glossy surface that so many of these paintings have, has presented problems of analysis, and suggests the use of wax treated with hot irons.

It is probably true that these are the three principal methods used: fresco (in the form of *stucco lustro*), encaustic and tempera. *Stucco lustro* required the careful preparation of the wall beforehand with successive layers of plaster over a roughened brick base. The final three or four coats were a fine plaster containing marble dust, and the last one was coloured. The colours used, according to Pliny, were earth and mineral in origin, and they were ironed on to a wet ground without pressure, the medium used to bind them being a mixture of soap and potash. Most of these paintings were done *in situ,* but some of the more important central panels were painted upon an easel on wood and fixed later with iron clamps. Few of the latter have survived owing to the rotting of the wood. The painting was coated with wax as a protection six weeks after it was finished.

The encaustic method is known incompletely, the formula having been lost in the Middle Ages. Pliny has, however, left some guiding information which indicates that the colour was applied either with hot wax, which hardened as it cooled, or as a cold paste, which was inusted later with a heated spatula. The quality of this method is extreme durability combined with freshness and liveliness of colour which does not darken or change with time. Evidence of this is provided by the Fayum mummy portraits from Egypt which date from the 1st century A. D.

Tempera is essentially the use of an emulsion as the binding medium of the colour to its ground, but in Pompeii, as elsewhere, the term included what is more accurately described as distemper, the colour here being bound with a glue. This method is not very permanent and is very susceptible to damp; thus it was only used for the cheaper work in the poorer houses and where a quick inexpensive method of limited durability was required.

Mosaic

The technique of mosaic consists of embedding small pieces of stone or glass, called tesserae, in cement. The cement was a Roman lime mortar to which thickened oils were added to slow down the cement's setting while making it actually thicker to the consistency of fondu. This gave the artist time in which to work while ensuring enough support for the tesserae as he pushed them in over a drawing. The Romans used tesserae mainly of opaque stone and pottery. The Byzantines later made use of the Eastern invention of coloured glass.